D1076444

FIND
THE
PRINCESS

igloobooks

M--T TH- PRIN------!

Ten little princesses are hiding on every page in this fun book!
Read the profiles below to learn all about each of your new royal friends. Then, look carefully at the scenes to try and find where they are all hiding. The answers are at the back of the book so you can check your searching skills.

NADIA

FAVOURITE HOBBY:
Horse riding

DISLIKES:
Carriages that turn into pumpkins

FAVOURITE COLOUR:
Purple

FLEUR

BIGGEST DREAM:
To be a ballerina

LOVES:
Playing video games

GOOD AT:
Putting tu and tu together

EILIDH

BIGGEST DREAM:
To own a huge library

FAVOURITE FOOD:
Gingerbread houses and candy canes

KNOWN FOR:
Taking a book everywhere

ELLA

FAVOURITE SNACK:
Tea-ara and biscuits

KNOWN FOR:
Always losing a shoe

FAVOURITE GAME:
Fairy chess

ROSE

WANTS TO:
Be a scientist

FAVOURITE THING TO DO:
Invent magical machines

MOST-LOVED ACCESSORY:
Flower crown

ZAINAB

FAVOURITE SPORT:
Dragon football

LIKES:
Ballgames and ballgowns

DREAMS OF:
Flying on a magic carpet

HARMONY

SECRET TALENT:
Playing electric guitar

FAVOURITE DRINK:
Strawberry milkshake

FAVOURITE THING TO DO:
Listen to music

LILLY

FAVOURITE HOBBY:
Making toy planes

BIGGEST DREAM:
To grow her hair really long

SECRET TALENT:
Juggling

ISABEL

ALWAYS WEARS:
Dungarees

DREAMS OF:
Climbing a magic beanstalk

SECRET TALENT:
Photography

AMBER

BIGGEST GOAL:
To be an ice-skating star

MOST-EATEN SNACK:
Palace popcorn

FAVOURITE COLOUR:
Ice blue

PERFECT PALACE

There's lots happening at the palace! Can you find all ten of your princess friends from the previous page?

CAN YOU SPOT THE BLUE STRAWBERRY?

PRINCESSES ON ICE

The princesses love dancing across the ice at the royal rink. Where are they all hiding?

CAN YOU SPOT THE PINK MUG?

FACTORY FUN

The chocolate factory is full of yummy snacks
to try! Can you spot all ten princesses?

CAN YOU SPOT THE GREEN HAT?

FAIREST OF THEM ALL

A day out at the fair is the perfect royal treat!
There are ten princesses hiding. Can you see where?

ROYAL TOWN

There's so much to see in the busy shopping street.
Search for the hiding places of all ten princesses.

Princess
PLANTS

CAN YOU SPOT THE RED CROWN?

OCEAN KINGDOM

The princesses love exploring under the sea.
Look carefully and try to find them all.

CAN YOU SPOT THE BLUE CRAB?

PRETTY PARK

The park is full of picnics, ice creams and games!
Find all ten princesses in the sunny scene.

CAN YOU SPOT
THE YELLOW
SKATEBOARD?

SPORTY SEARCH

It's time for a royal sports day! Can you spot
all the princesses playing hide-and-seek?

CAN YOU SPOT THE BLUE CONE?

LOST IN THE JUNGLE

Ten princesses are exploring in the jungle.
Where are they hiding? Find them all!

CAN YOU SPOT THE RED SPIDER?

GINGERBREAD CASTLE

This magical candyland is full of yummy treats!
Look closely to find all ten princesses.